THE PROBLEM WITH THE MALE GAZE

The Problem with the Male Gaze

Liz Fe Lifestyle

Published by Liz Fe Lifestyle
Columbus, Oh 43223

The Problem with the Male Gaze
Copyright 2023 by Liz Fe Lifestyle

Cover, layout, and design by Liz Fe Lifestyle.

All rights reserved. No part of this book may be reproduced in any form or by any electronic or mechanical means, including information storage and retrieval systems, without written permission from the author and the original publisher, except in the case of a reviewer, who may quote brief passages embodied in critical articles or in a review.

This publication is designed to provide accurate and authoritative information in regard to the subject matter covered. It is sold with the understanding that the publisher is not engaged in rendering legal, accounting, or other professional service. If legal advice or other expert assistance is required, the services of a competent professional person should be sought.

Manufactured in the United States of America

About the Publisher

Who Are We?

Liz Fe Lifestyle Publishing was founded in 2017 and is headquartered in Columbus, OH. We publish books with women empowerment in mind. We're a BIPOC, women-owned book publishing company based in Columbus, Ohio.

Who Are We Here For?

For those who are uniquely interested in books by women, for women.

What Is Our Social Cause?

We believe in being a force for good. We empower women with our content by writing books such as, The Problem with the Male Gaze and its sequel, The Toxic Female Gaze, that are geared toward educating and empowering women. We believe in making a real impact and spreading awareness about the real threats women face every day.

"A 2018 analysis of prevalence data from 2000-2018 across 161 countries and areas, conducted by WHO on behalf of the UN Interagency working group on violence against women, found that worldwide, nearly 1 in 3, or 30%, of women have been subjected to physical and/or sexual violence by an intimate partner or non-partner sexual violence or both."

- World Health Organization

Table of Contents

Introduction   1

Chapter 1: What is the Male Gaze?   6

Chapter 2: The Male Gaze in Classrooms   11

Chapter 3: In-Depth Examples of the Male Gaze in Media   19

Chapter 4: Nina Menkes: Taking on the Male Gaze in Film   30

Chapter 5: The Role of Social Media   34

Chapter 6: The Psychological and Societal Effects   38

Chapter 7: Breaking Down Stereotypes and Counter-Narratives   42

Chapter 8: The Era of the Me Too Movement   46

Chapter 9: The Role of Feminism and Activism   50

Chapter 10: Fetishizing Women   54

Chapter 11: Beyond Gender: Intersectionality and the Male Gaze — 58

Chapter 12: Redefining Masculinity — 60

Chapter 13: The Future of Representation — 64

Chapter 14: The Female Gaze — 68

Chapter 15: A Gaze into the Future - Breaking Free from the Shackles of the Male Gaze — 73

The Bottom Line — 77

Acknowledgments — 79

Appendix — 82

References — 86

Dear Reader — 90

Introduction

In a world where art, media, and culture continually shape our perceptions and attitudes, the concept of the "male gaze" looms large. It's a concept that has subtly, yet profoundly, influenced the way we see the world, ourselves, and each other. The male gaze is not just a theoretical construct; it is a pervasive force that has been etched into our collective consciousness, defining and limiting the ways we understand gender, power, and representation.

This book, "The Problem with the Male Gaze," embarks on a journey to dissect, critique, and ultimately transcend this powerful construct. The male gaze, as first articulated by film critic Laura Mulvey in her 1975 essay "Visual Pleasure and Narrative Cinema," describes a phenomenon where women are portrayed and perceived primarily as objects of male desire within visual culture. Mulvey's seminal work drew attention to the dominant and often objectifying ways in which women were presented in cinema, a critique that later extended to various forms of media and art.

The male gaze is rooted in the history of art and storytelling, where women have frequently been depicted through the eyes of male artists and writers. It has played a foundational role in shaping not only how women are portrayed but also how they are expected to behave and perceive themselves.

Yet, it's essential to acknowledge that the male gaze does not operate in isolation; it is part of a complex web of intersecting systems of power, privilege, and oppression. It reinforces harmful stereotypes, perpetuates gender inequalities, and contributes to a culture that often objectifies and commodifies women.

Our exploration of the male gaze is not an attempt to vilify men or male perspectives, nor is it a simplistic condemnation of all male-created art or media. Instead, this book seeks to foster a deeper understanding of how the male gaze operates, its multifaceted impact on society, and the possibilities for transformation and change. It recognizes that the male gaze is not solely a "men vs. women" issue but a systemic challenge that requires collective awareness and action to overcome.

Why is it crucial to confront the male gaze in the 21st century? The answer lies in the enduring power of visual culture to shape our beliefs, behaviors, and values. Media, art, and popular culture are not passive mirrors reflecting society; they are active agents in constructing and reinforcing our worldview. They inform how we perceive our own bodies, identities, and relationships, influencing everything from our self-esteem to our attitudes towards others.

Consider the countless advertisements, films, TV shows, and magazines that bombard us daily. How often are women presented as passive objects of desire, their worth measured by their appearance and their ability to fulfill male fantasies? How often are men portrayed as dominant, emotionally distant figures, reinforced by toxic ideals of masculinity? The male gaze is an inescapable presence in this visual landscape, perpetuating gender norms that harm both women and men.

The male gaze is not confined to traditional media. The digital age has amplified its reach and impact. Social media platforms, where individuals curate their online personas, are often breeding grounds for the male gaze. The pressure to present oneself as attractive, desirable, and conforming to narrow beauty standards is palpable, with serious consequences for mental health and self-esteem.

Moreover, the male gaze is not solely a gender issue; it intersects with race, sexuality, class, and other dimensions of identity. Women of color face unique challenges when it comes to representation and the impact of the male gaze. Our exploration will delve into these intersectional dynamics, recognizing that no one is exempt from its influence, and no one is powerless to challenge it.

The significance of addressing the male gaze in the 21st century cannot be overstated. As we confront pressing issues related to gender equality, diversity, and inclusivity, understanding and dismantling the male gaze becomes an essential part of the broader struggle for a more just and equitable world. It is a call to action for artists, media creators, consumers, educators, activists, and all individuals who believe in the power of representation to shape our shared reality.

In the pages that follow, we will embark on a multidimensional journey through history, psychology, art, media, feminism, and activism. We will examine case studies, engage with diverse voices, and explore the strategies and initiatives that challenge the male gaze. This book is an invitation to join a critical conversation, to question the status quo, and to envision a world where representation reflects the complexity and diversity of human experiences, free from the constraints of the male gaze. It is a call to collectively unveil the gaze, challenge its hold on our culture, and illuminate a path toward a more inclusive and liberated future.

The male gaze is not confined to traditional media. The digital age has amplified its reach and impact. Social media platforms, where individuals curate their online personas, are often breeding grounds for the male gaze. The pressure to present oneself as attractive, desirable, and conforming to narrow beauty standards is palpable, with serious consequences for mental health and self-esteem.

Moreover, the male gaze is not solely a gender issue; it intersects with race, sexuality, class, and other dimensions of identity. Women of color face unique challenges when it comes to representation and the impact of the male gaze. Our exploration will delve into these intersectional dynamics, recognizing that no one is exempt from its influence, and no one is powerless to challenge it.

The significance of addressing the male gaze in the 21st century cannot be overstated. As we confront pressing issues related to gender equality, diversity, and inclusivity, understanding and dismantling the male gaze becomes an essential part of the broader struggle for a more just and equitable world. It is a call to action for artists, media creators, consumers, educators, activists, and all individuals who believe in the power of representation to shape our shared reality.

In the pages that follow, we will embark on a multidimensional journey through history, psychology, art, media, feminism, and activism. We will examine case studies, engage with diverse voices, and explore the strategies and initiatives that challenge the male gaze. This book is an invitation to join a critical conversation, to question the status quo, and to envision a world where representation reflects the complexity and diversity of human experiences, free from the constraints of the male gaze.

It is a call to collectively unveil the gaze, challenge its hold on our culture, and illuminate a path toward a more inclusive and liberated future.

Chapter 1:
What is the Male Gaze?

The term "Male Gaze" was coined by Laura Mulvey in the year 1975. Mulvey is a feminist film theorist from Britain. In her renowned 1973 essay, Visual Pleasure and Narrative Cinema, Mulvey, who is also a professor of film and media studies at the University of London, describes the concept of the male gaze. She discusses the theory of sexually objectifying women in media from a heterosexual man's point of view. For a majority of the entertainment industry, women are shown as docile objects of male desire. In terms of the psychological reasoning behind the male gaze, it is similar to the Freudian concept of scopophilia – the pleasure of looking.

Mulvey is a prominent film theorist in the industry and her ideas bring awareness to cases of clear misogyny in films and other forms of media. Her theory has allowed people to start questioning gender roles in films and how they propagate false realities in the name of fiction. It has been decades since she called out films and media for their wrongdoings, yet our entertainment industry still thrives on sexually objectifying women and placing them in traditional roles.

> *"...the gender power asymmetry is a controlling force in cinema and constructed for the pleasure of the male viewer, which is deeply rooted in patriarchal ideologies and discourses,"* says Mulvey.

A majority of these scenes are targeted towards a male audience, so everything is catered to their liking. The root cause for this issue stems from a male-driven society that views women as their property and inferiors. This theory that Mulvey developed and studied is just as relevant in the 21st century as it was back in 1975.

According to her, the roles that are written for women are often meant to simply bear meaning, a symbol of sorts pertaining to a male storyline. These characters never take control of a scene, as they are seen as mere embellishments. Their purpose is to just stand in the frame and look pretty while the men in that room and in the audience gawk at them to please themselves. What is so extremely frustrating about this concept is that the roles are never really reversed. It is quite rare to see men in the same position. This disparity just goes on to reinforce the idea that women are eye candy and men have the right to treat them in that way.

As Budd Boetticher, who directed classic Western films in the 1950s, puts it: "What counts is what the heroine provokes, or rather what she represents. She is the one, or rather the love or fear she inspires in the hero, or else the concern he feels for her, who makes him act the way he does. In herself the woman has not the slightest importance."

The Birth of the Male Gaze

In the intricate tapestry of human history and culture, there exist threads woven so deeply that they continue to shape our perceptions, values, and interactions. One such thread is the concept of the male gaze, a phenomenon rooted in the annals of art and literature that has, for centuries, molded our understanding of gender, sexuality, and power dynamics. To comprehend the contemporary problem of the male gaze, we must journey back to its origins, unravel its historical implications, and dissect the ways it has persisted into our modern world.

The Historical Roots

The male gaze, as a concept, finds its roots in the artistic and literary traditions of the Western world. Ancient civilizations celebrated the human form in art, but it was during the Renaissance period that the male gaze began to take a distinctive form. Renaissance artists, influenced by the revival of classical ideals, often depicted the female body as an object of beauty and desire. Paintings, sculptures, and literature from this era frequently cast women as passive, sensual beings, existing primarily for the pleasure and consumption of the male viewer.

Leonardo da Vinci's iconic masterpiece, the "Mona Lisa," exemplifies this early manifestation of the male gaze. While the painting's enigmatic smile is celebrated, it also objectifies the subject, reducing her to an alluring image for the male viewer's contemplation. In literature, the works of authors like Geoffrey Chaucer and Boccaccio often featured female characters as objects of male desire, reinforcing the idea that women were passive vessels for male fantasies.

Shaping Early Perceptions of Women

The male gaze, in its infancy, not only affected artistic and literary representations but also seeped into broader societal norms. It reinforced gender roles and expectations, casting women as objects to be admired and desired, while men were positioned as the active subjects of desire and agency. This dynamic found expression not only in art but in the everyday lives of people, influencing their expectations, behaviors, and relationships.

For example, the practice of corseting, which constrained women's bodies into an exaggerated hourglass shape, exemplified the physical embodiment of the male gaze. Women contorted their bodies to fit a societal ideal of beauty, often at the expense of their health, all in the pursuit of conforming to male expectations of attractiveness. These physical manifestations of the male gaze underscored its pervasive influence on women's lives.

The Shifting Landscape of the Male Gaze

As time marched forward, the male gaze continued to evolve. The advent of photography in the 19th century and the subsequent rise of cinema in the 20th century brought new dimensions to the gaze. Photography allowed for the widespread circulation of images, while cinema introduced motion and narrative, both of which could be harnessed to convey and reinforce gendered stereotypes.

In the early days of cinema, female characters were often relegated to two-dimensional roles: the damsel in distress or the object of desire. These representations served to perpetuate the idea that women existed primarily in relation to men, either as helpless victims awaiting rescue or as objects to be won. Icons like Marilyn Monroe became symbols of this era, celebrated for their physical beauty but rarely recognized for their talents or agency.

As we trace the history of the male gaze, it becomes evident that its evolution has been a complex interplay between art, literature, societal norms, and technological advancements. In Chapter 3, we will delve further into how the male gaze transitioned from traditional art to modern media, solidifying its presence in contemporary culture.

Chapter 2:
The Male Gaze in Classrooms

The teachings of catering to the male gaze start early on, particularly in educational settings like the classroom. When students go to school, they not only learn the ins and outs of the multiplication table and the steps on how to draft an essay, they also learn that women are objects of pleasure that exist solely for the men to take. This can be seen during times when boys chase girls outside at recess just for the fun of it, even though the girls may view the chase as an unwanted pursuit.

Patriarchal values can also be seen in action when teachers brush off the fact that a girl is being bullied by a boy, dealing with the matter by simply stating that "boys will be boys." It is well known that boys who exhibit mean behavior toward girls tend to have crushes on them. However, the failure of teachers to curb this kind of toxic behavior at a young age will only serve to harm women more severely later on in life. Boys will grow up believing that acting harshly and cruelly is an acceptable way to treat women.

Gender based violence that takes place in school settings is a major obstacle to universal schooling and the right to education for girls. Globally, one in three students, aged 11–15, have been bullied by their peers at school at least once in their lives, if not more.

While boys are more likely to experience physical bullying than girls, girls are more likely to experience psychological bullying, which can be just as harmful or even more damaging than physical bullying.

Psychological bullying is described as purposeful and intentional mental abuse that can include making jokes or spreading false rumors and lies about someone. Those who have endured psychological bullying can have emotional problems that linger long after the abuse has happened. Girls report being made fun of because of how their face or body looks more frequently than boys.

Furthermore, there are the established school dress codes that zero in on girls' bodies while boys' bodies are more or less exempt from such careful critiquing. Girls' shoulders are too scandalous, their knees are distractions toward learning, and wearing leggings and yoga pants is strictly off limits.

Girls are taught to adjust themselves to fit into a man's world and made to feel that there is something wrong with their bodies when they are embarrassingly enough, sent home from school to change into something more "modest."

The most common figures of authority roaming the school halls are cis, white, heterosexual, middle class, male teachers. According to federal data, 79 percent of male teachers represent this ideal.

Because the majority of teachers identify themselves as fitting within these categories, they possess the mindset and ability to exact the authority necessary to maintain a standard of strict dress coding that is acceptable to their eyes, aka the male gaze. To women and girls, life is a constant struggle of creating a routine to protect themselves whether it is from danger, embarrassment or whatnot.

> *"Women negotiate unsafe spaces through avoidance, protection, and prevention."*
> *-Sanghamitra Roy, ScienceDirect*

Schoolgirls may avoid wearing their favorite skirt for fear of enduring the embarrassment of being singled out and told to change again. Women avoid traveling alone or going out at certain times of the day to prevent being attacked or kidnapped while men face much less risk when going out by themselves at late hours. One out of ten girls already experience incidents of catcalling before they even reach their eleventh birthdays.

School dress codes perpetuate the notion that wearing clothing pieces such as spaghetti strap tank tops and yoga pants are cause for men to exact abuse upon them, that women are "asking for it." In reality, it's not about the type of clothing a woman wears, but the inability of men to control themselves and view women as something other than objects. The fact that young girls who have not even reached middle school yet are being sexualized is something that should not be happening. If anything, it seems to give the impression that dress codes are in place to prevent adult male teachers from becoming distracted or tempted by girls' bodies.

At an elementary school age, both boys and girls are at a similar stage of bodily development, so they mostly view each other in a manner devoid of anything sexual. Therefore, many schools' reasoning for implementing a dress code targeting girls, which is that girls' body parts are distracting to the boys, is false and in fact, has everything to do with the male staff working at the schools and nothing to do with the boy students. Dress codes are also still in existence simply for the purpose of oppressing the female population and upholding an outdated standard for women.

At the Tokyo 2020 Olympics, the German women's gymnastics team chose to do something out of the ordinary and protested against sexualization by wearing unitards that offered full coverage. Instead of the bikini cut of traditional leotards, their outfits consisted of ankle length pants. The legs of traditional leotards, which are extremely high-cut, are meant to make women's legs look longer, more elegant, and most important of all, more appealing to the male gaze. The outfits enhance the aesthetic of the performance for the judges and the spectators without taking into consideration the extreme discomfort these types of leotards cause. Clothing for male gymnasts consists of much less revealing attire, with the usual outfit being a singlet accompanied with loose shorts.

This also is not the first time that the German women's gymnastics team dabbled in the concept of pushing the boundaries of sexist male oriented principles. A German gymnast named Sarah Voss wore a unitard that fully covered her whole body during the European Artistic Gymnastics Championship in Basel, Switzerland which took place back in April of 2021. Voss explained that she wants to help young women feel more comfortable continuing a career in gymnastics. She revealed that many girls quit the sport because of the stress of worrying about appearances.

"To do splits and jumps, sometimes the leotards are not covering everything, sometimes they slip and that's why we invented a new form of leotard so that everyone feels safe around competitions and training. Every time you don't feel safe it's distracting you from what you want to perform.
-Sarah Voss, Sports.yahoo.com

The standard leotard lacks comfort and coverage; it especially is not suitable for times when the athletes must deal with their menstrual cycles. Women do not need to be punished for doing or wearing what helps to alleviate their discomfort during a natural physiological process that is completely out of their control. (No, women cannot just "hold it in.") This just leads to women developing an unhealthy relationship with their bodies and creates unnecessary anxiety over menstrual cycles when there is already such a stigma surrounding periods.

> *"We women all want to feel good in our skin...As a little girl I didn't see the tight gym outfits as such a big deal. But when puberty began, when my period came, I began feeling increasingly uncomfortable."*
> *-Sarah Voss*

The strict dress codes for female athletes almost seems like a way to punish women for not being men. The German women's gymnastics team strives to inspire other female gymnasts and athletes in different fields by showing them that they should be able to wear whatever they want to help them perform to the best of their abilities, whether it be something more revealing or completely full-coverage. The common argument for female athletes wearing more revealing clothing is that it helps them perform better and gives them free-ranging mobility; however, men wear clothing that gives them more coverage, yet they still perform well. At this point, it is clear that the issue is not about mobility.

The policing of female athletes' bodies does not end with the gymnastics team. Black women on the Olympic swim team must face an additional set of barriers that they have to overcome.

Much of this has to do with who exactly is behind the scenes. Straight white men have created 95 percent of the cinematic images we've ever seen in American mainstream films. They have made all the decisions leading up to the finished product–the shots, the framing, the lighting, the design of movie images in general. According to *Variety*, out of the 1,447 directors responsible for the most popular films over the past decade, only 4.8 percent were women, 6.1 percent were Black, 3.3 percent were Asian and 3.7 percent were Hispanic/Latino.

The impact of film is so powerful and so ubiquitous that white men's perspective has been normalized and they have shaped their worldview to being considered the one true, valid version of real life that everyone sees and experiences, but it actually is not. It is only one pair of lenses which we are all being forced to look through. Stacy L. Smith, founder of the USC Annenberg Inclusion Initiative, speculates on the lack of diversity in the film industry and how that reflects on the real world itself: "There doesn't seem to be a real policy or process of creating an ecosystem of inclusion on screen. It's remarkable how resistant to change the industry is. When you look at the whole ecosystem, things really haven't budged."

I am going to ask you to pause for a second and think of the last movie or show or music video you saw and how the female actresses were portrayed in that medium. What was the point of view? What parts of the women were given the most screen time?

To give you a brief example, a 1950s advertisement from the coffee brand Chase and Sanborn depicts a woman draped over a man's lap while the man's hand is raised mid-air, where he is clearly about to spank her. This outrageously sexist ad was meant to show the "pressure packed power" of the coffee.

The 1950s was notorious for its culture of sexism, but that was decades ago and hints of those same kinds of references can still be seen today, years later.

In 2020, KFC aired an ad in Australia that showed two young boys gawking at a woman's breasts, upholding the outdated idea that "boys will be boys" and trying to profit off of the mentality that "sex sells." Many people took to social media to express their outrage over the fried chicken franchise's sexist depiction of women. KFC issued an apology for their ad, and rightfully so; however, it was pointed out by several individuals that KFC would never have taken accountability for their actions if not for the amount of criticism that landed them in hot water.

Abhik Roy, a former ad executive and professor of marketing at Quinnipiac University, told The New York Times in an interview that, "they [KFC] would have never apologized 15 or 20 years ago; it's more because of social media pressure." This example shows that although progress has been made, with plenty of people willing to speak up and call out questionable behavior, there is still work to be done, as it is all too easy for companies and organizations run by majority cis/het white men to regress backwards to tired, overused stereotypes.

Mulvey wrote that in the media, a woman is a spectacle and the man is "the bearer of the look." Let's look at the 2005 film The Duke of Hazzard, for instance, when Daisy Duke (Jessica Simpson) enters the scene in a long trench coat only to remove it to reveal nothing but a pink bikini underneath. This scene is a wide shot, so Daisy's entire body is on display for the male characters and the male audience. As she walks toward the camera, it is almost as if she is breaking the fourth wall, essentially letting the male audience stare at her all they want.

"Visual media that respond to masculine voyeurism will tend to sexualize women for a male viewer as well as the male characters being depicted on the screen," says Garner.

Now some of you may be thinking that men go through the same in shirtless scenes and such. But let me stop you right there. A shirtless scene of a man is not always about the female audience. It is about the man being proud of his body and looks because he believes that women, much like most men, only care about the physical appearance of their partner. For the shirtless man, he knows what he is doing and the effect it has on those around him. Despite being shirtless or even naked, he will still be in control over his female counterpart in that scene. For women, that is not the case because they are presented as objects.

Mulvey argues, "the male figure cannot bear the burden of sexual objectification. Man is reluctant to gaze."

Just take Patty Jenkins's Wonder Woman as an example. There is a scene where Chris Pine's character Steve Trevor is naked on screen, but there is an important reason behind it. In this scene, Trevor's nudity is a part of the plot as he is still actively participating in the scene. Unlike Daisy Duke, he is not breaking the fourth wall by putting himself on display.

Especially when it comes to action based films like James Bond and Transformers, the female characters, no matter who they are, are viewed from the male gaze.

For the majority of the time, their main purpose within the plot is to feed the sexual interest or satisfy the sexual agenda of the male characters. Female characters often wear high heeled shoes, tight clothing, and always have perfectly long, flowing hair that is let down even in fight scenes.

Many of the female protagonists, specifically, are not given the agency they deserve and are therefore referred to as the "fighting fuck toy" trope. This term was coined by Caroline Heldman and it is used to describe hypersexualized female protagonists who fight alongside the male protagonists and look good while doing it.

"The FFT appears empowered, but her very existence serves the pleasure of the heterosexual male viewer, says Heldman. "In short, the FFT takes female agency, weds it to normalized male violence, and appropriates it for the male gaze."

Ridley Scott's *Alien* is another example of Mulvey's theory. Despite its controversial classification as a feminist film, it does conform to Mulvey's claim of the male gaze. While the women are not heavily shown as erotic or objective, the first part of the film is a "split between the active male and the passive female" in the first portion of the film. Dallas, the main character, makes all of the key decisions throughout. Within his company, he is given power over his crew, the one who is "free to command the stage…who "articulates the look and creates the action."

Another example is through the Disney Princesses, such as Snow White and Sleeping Beauty, of the popular Disney franchise through their plots and storylines.

Mulvey's theory applies itself through the eyes of the woman and indicates that they're happy only when they fall in love with man, suggesting to the audience of Disney, which consists of mainly impressionable children and girls, that they will only be happy when they fall in love. This implies that men are the only answers for these princess characters, and the solution to their own happiness. Most of their stories do not end with them being alone and feeling good with their decision (Elsa being the recent exception). The men/princes are shown as heroic brave characters while the princesses are captured and waiting helplessly to be saved.

There is also Dennis Villineuve's 2017 film Blade Runner 2049 starring Ryan Gosling. The film takes the idea of women as objects to a whole new level. The main female character in the film is not even a human, but a technological being that shows up when commanded by Ryan Gosling's character. It also appears in whatever form he desires, whether that be a maid or a housewife. One of the other main female characters in the film is a large, naked female hologram that does not have any eyeballs. Eyes are often called the "windows to the soul, " so what does it imply when this female character does not seem to have any?

The way men are typically shot and depicted in movies bring out their most human characteristics. We can see the barely noticeable wrinkles at the corners of their eyes, their slightly crooked smile, maybe even a tiny freckle on the side of their cheek. These small details show viewers the depth and reality of the characters' personalities. Women on the other hand, are often devoid of humanity. Their faces are usually free of wrinkles or other unique identifying marks, having flawless porcelain skin instead with not a hair out of place. They are portrayed as flat, unrelatable characters without a tidbit of personality or unique trait that lets viewers know she is someone truly important and relevant to the film.

Close-up shots of women tend to zoom in on body parts more than anything else.

> *"The FFT appears empowered, but her very existence serves the pleasure of the heterosexual male viewer, says Heldman. "In short, the FFT takes female agency, weds it to normalized male violence, and appropriates it for the male gaze."*
> *-Director Numa Perrier, Variety*

The 2020 box office hit Hustlers, starring Constance Wu and Jennifer Lopez, manages to successfully avoid portraying women as one dimensional characters. Written and directed by Lorene Scafaria, a woman, the film follows a group of strippers who scammed their clients from Wall Street after the recession of 2008. Although the film is about strippers, women who have been traditionally objectified solely for their bodies, it actually does a good job putting the women at the center and focusing on their complicated stories, issues and accomplishments. The film also does not depict the women's bodies in an objectifying manner.

Additionally, films like *Frozen* and *Suffragette* promote women's independence and empowerment based on Mulvey's theory. There are films such as *The Wolf of Wall Street* who promote women in sexually unnecessary manners. One reason is because men dominate the film industry, making Mulvey's critical analysis of the film industry all the more urgent. Producers were willing to create the same work because it brought pleasure to the audience, and most importantly, it elevated profits. Doing this will give the audience what they want, but not many women or other marginalized communities believe this to be true.

This methodation would only satisfy the white male audience and exclude the rest of society.

With the shift of incredibly sexist television shows and movies to films that depict less objectification, how does this teach self-worth to young girls and other women? What does this help them strive for?

From Art to Media - The Pervasiveness of the Male Gaze

In a previous chapter, we explored the historical origins of the male gaze, tracing its roots in art and literature. However, the male gaze did not remain confined to the canvas and the written word. Instead, it has evolved and proliferated in the modern world through various media forms, leaving an indelible mark on our collective consciousness. This chapter delves into the transition of the male gaze from traditional art to contemporary media and highlights its pervasive nature in advertising, film, television, and the internet.

The Transition from Canvas to Screen

As the 20th century dawned, art was not the sole realm where the male gaze held sway. The emergence of new technologies, particularly photography and film, allowed for the replication and dissemination of images on an unprecedented scale. Artists and filmmakers alike were presented with an opportunity to capture and convey their perspectives to a broader audience.

In cinema, the male gaze became particularly pronounced. Hollywood, in its early days, was dominated by male directors and producers who perpetuated traditional gender roles and norms. Actresses were often cast based on their physical attractiveness, and their characters were molded to cater to the male viewer's desires. The camera itself became an extension of the male gaze, objectifying women on screen through lingering shots, suggestive framing, and voyeuristic angles.

Advertising: Selling More Than Just Products

One of the most pervasive and influential arenas where the male gaze thrives is advertising.

Advertisements shape our desires, aspirations, and perceptions of beauty and success. Through the lens of the male gaze, women have frequently been depicted as passive objects of desire, existing primarily to attract male attention. This portrayal not only reinforces harmful stereotypes but also links the consumption of products with sexual conquest.

Consider the countless advertisements where scantily clad women are used to sell everything from cars to hamburgers. These images not only objectify women but also send a clear message that their primary value lies in their ability to titillate and entice. The male gaze in advertising normalizes and perpetuates unrealistic beauty standards, which can have profound psychological and emotional effects on individuals, both male and female.

Film and Television: Shaping Our Perceptions

The male gaze's influence extends beyond advertising and infiltrates our entertainment choices. In the world of film and television, the male gaze has a significant impact on storytelling and character development. Female characters are often reduced to one-dimensional stereotypes, their story arcs revolving around their relationships with male protagonists or their physical appearance.

Moreover, the disparity in behind-the-scenes representation exacerbates the problem. The lack of female directors, writers, and producers means that the male perspective often dominates the creative process. This lack of diversity in storytelling perpetuates harmful gender dynamics and limits the narratives available to audiences.

The Digital Age: The Male Gaze on the Internet

The advent of the internet and digital media has further amplified the male gaze's reach and influence. Social media platforms, where users curate and share their own content, have created spaces where the male gaze can thrive unchecked. The constant stream of images and videos on platforms like Instagram, TikTok, and YouTube has given rise to a culture of instant gratification and superficial judgments based on physical appearance.

Cyberbullying, online harassment, and the dissemination of explicit content without consent are all manifestations of the male gaze in the digital age. Women and marginalized communities are disproportionately affected, as their online presence is often met with objectification and harassment.

The male gaze, which originated in the world of art, has seamlessly transitioned into the modern media landscape. It shapes our perceptions of gender, beauty, and relationships, influencing how we view ourselves and others. The next chapters will delve into the psychological and societal effects of the male gaze, and explore strategies for challenging and dismantling this pervasive phenomenon.

Chapter 4:
Nina Menkes: Taking on the Male Gaze in Film

Nina Menkes is a first generation independent feminist filmmaker, born to European Jews who fled from Nazi persecution. Her family history is filled with trauma, violence, alienation and murder, all of which is central to her work. Her films include *The Great Sadness of Zohara* (1983), *Magdalena Viraga* (1986), *Queen of Diamonds* (1991), *The Bloody Child* (1996), *Phantom Love* (2007), and *Dissolution* (2010). Menkes was born in Ann Arbor, Michigan and received her bachelor's degree from the University of California at Berkeley. She later completed a Master of Fine Arts in 1987 at the University of California at Los Angeles. Menkes now teaches at the California Institute of the Arts in Santa Clarita, California.

Menkes became a more prominent figure in the film industry after publishing her article in Filmmaker Magazine in 2018 shortly after the Harvey Weinstein scandal broke out. The article is titled, *The Visual Language of Oppression: Harvey Wasn't Working in a Vacuum*. It details the relationship between the conventions of visual culture and the culture of sexual assault and victim blaming in Hollywood. Menkes writes, "An entire culture of visual language supports and encourages this system, justifying both the perpetrators' actions and the victims' humiliated silence.

It is essential that this visual code of oppression be exposed and understood. Demoting half the world's population to use-objects happens not only at the level of script and narrative but within actual framing choices and lighting strategies."

In 2020, Menkes presented a live lecture called Sex and Power: The Visual Language of Oppression, a fuller version of the snippets she provided in her preview, the article. This presentation grew out of her many experiences with film and lectures in the classroom. She has given this live presentation to universities and high profile film festivals all over the world. Her lecture is about diving deeper into techniques utilized by Hollywood cinema to reinforce a culture of misogyny.

Menkes' talk consists of six main points, which have now been dubbed The Menkes List. Viewers can utilize the list to help them spot these techniques used for the women on screen and compare whether or not the same techniques are being used for the men. The list includes male point of view: female is the object, fragmented body parts, camera movement: pans and tilts, two dimensional or other fantasy lighting, disconnected from the narrative space, and a slow motion camera speed. Menkes hopes to raise awareness of the issue and prompt people to think deeper about the way women appear in film and television. The Wexner Center describes the lecture like this:

"Using film clips from the golden age of Hollywood to the present (including films by Martin Scorsese, Spike Lee, Alfred Hitchcock, and many others), she shows how ideas about women have become unconsciously embedded in our heads by the visual language of cinema—through lighting, framing, camera angles, and movement—and how these contribute to sexual intimidation and discrimination."

-Syracuse University

Ever since then, Menkes has been working on a documentary called Brainwashed. The documentary will outline cinematic techniques that objectify women and girls and will build upon Menkes's presentation. It also touches on films from the 1940s all the way to modern day movies. Menkes is both directing and producing the film and is collaborating with a mostly female team. She is also aware that even female filmmakers and cinematographers can fall victim to sexualizing the female body. This is part of the reason why she is so passionate about getting the word out.

"I've had women students come in and show footage that begins on the woman character's face, then for no apparent reason it cuts down to her low-cut shirt. And goes lower. And then back up. And I'd say, 'Why did you film that way?' And there'd be this deer-in-the-headlights look. They were doing what they'd seen a million times. And weren't even aware of it. Heterosexual male actors are almost never filmed that way."

Menkes holds many honors and awards. These awards include a Los Angeles Film Critics Association Award, a Guggenheim Fellowship, two fellowships from the National Endowment for the Arts and much more. Menkes was one of the first women to ever present a feature film at the Sundance Film Festival (Queen of Diamonds.) Her film, The Bloody Child was deemed one of the most important and influential films in the past 50 years by the Viennale International Film Festival in Austria. Two of Menkes's films have also been chosen by the Academy Film Archive and Scorsese's Film Foundation for restoration. Queen of Diamonds was re-released in 2019 and was considered a big hit. It is widely regarded as "a modern masterpiece."

Chapter 5:
The Role of Social Media

Living under the male gaze, the constant objectification of women and girls, the seemingly never-ending scrutiny all play a part in how women go about their daily lives. Despite popular belief, it does more than change how a girl poses for a photo or determine what types of clothes women should wear. In the stark reality of it all, growing up around patriarchal values and being exposed to the male gaze, makes it take root into our very beings and controls the way we carry ourselves, our entire thought processes and even warps our own perspectives of ourselves.

Due to its rapid growth and extensive reach, social media and its respective networking sites have become a key element of the modern lifestyle. It has become a particularly convenient method for men to further expand the influence of the male gaze. Globally, internet users are spending about 1.97 hours per day on social networking sites, with individuals 16-24 years of age averaging 2.68 hours on social media sites such as Instagram. Models/influencers and celebrities like the Kardashians continue to reinforce unrealistic body images. Users who see positive comments from men or whoever else under these women's photos are motivated to follow in their footsteps.

It has been found that female social media users typically post more photos online than male users. Women also have a higher desire to present themselves as attractive and hold more importance toward aesthetically pleasing photos than men do. This recent obsession in one's appearance and receiving direct approval from others regarding appearances is frankly, a new breeding ground for sexual objectification of women to occur in.

> "As a society our image of beauty is consistent with what we see in advertisements. We perpetuate this image on a day to day basis on social media - the pictures we post, the filters we use, the people we follow align with how we see beauty. I think at the end of the day, companies...are selling an image of beauty and romance that the mass market aspires to have."
> -Christopher Manila, Marketing and Algebra Entrepreneurship teacher, Evanstonian.net

According to studies conducted by Tiggemann and Miller in 2010, the more time young adolescent girls spent on social networking sites, the more dissatisfaction they showed with their weight and the more they became riveted on the goal of being thin. Many other studies reveal that increasing cases of depression, anxiety, eating disorders, suicidal ideation, etc. among young women and girls are related to female objectification.

To touch on this topic a bit further, the rising popularity of the app TikTok emphasizes the disparities between men and women more than ever before. Young girls on the app dress in tighter, more revealing outfits while performing TikTok dances to gain more followers compared to young boys who do the same dances but donned in baggy clothing instead. It is not necessary for men to show off their bodies to gain more followers; they can acquire just as many as girls who flaunt their bodies. Girls who do not show any skin might not attain as many followers as boys who do not wear revealing clothes.

Big brands like Victoria's Secret have a lot of influence on consumers. The utilization of social media to promote their products and images causes the brand to be even more prominent. The lingerie company generated over $6.8 billion in 2019, their numbers truly revealing how massive of a reach the brand has. Recently, the brand's objectifying and misogynistic culture has been exposed by models brave enough to speak up about the experiences they have endured. For instance, Ed Razek, top executive of a parent company of Victoria's Secret, is known for his highly inappropriate behavior of trying to kiss models and have them sit on his lap. Model Andi Muise rejected Razek's advances and in return, she was never hired by the brand again.

Victoria's Secret is a brand that caters to women, yet their treatment of women, particularly their female models, is incredibly degrading and unacceptable. We again see the pattern of women being treated like objects because they are wearing revealing clothing, even though that is what they were hired to do. Victoria's Secret's treatment of their female employees sends the message that it is okay to continue objectifying women.

Just this year, Victoria's Secret has announced that they are planning to rebrand the company and shed its old image once and for all after years of consumer complaints about the brand's lack of inclusivity and diversity. Some are praising the brand for this much-needed move toward female empowerment, but many others are claiming that Victoria's Secret is merely following a trend and their rebranding has come too little, too late, fueled by pressure from social media. Becca Post, founder of the national branding agency Helen & Gertrude, says:

> *"So many brands are doing this as a reaction, rather than being a thought leader. Companies don't have to wait for a crisis to do a rebrand."*

Victoria's Secret themselves even admitted to The New York Times that they were "slow to respond" to changing times. Quite frankly, the brand's slowness seems to indicate a hearty reluctance to let go of outdated values and give women the respect they deserve. This is why brands like Victoria's Secret are so problematic.

Chapter 6: The Psychological and Societal Effects

The male gaze isn't merely a theoretical concept; it has tangible, far-reaching effects on both individuals and society as a whole. In this chapter, we delve into the psychological and societal ramifications of the male gaze, shedding light on its pervasive influence.

1. Shaping Perceptions of Gender Roles and Norms

The male gaze plays a crucial role in shaping societal perceptions of gender roles and norms. From an early age, individuals are exposed to media and art that reinforce traditional gender stereotypes. Women are often portrayed as passive objects of desire, while men are depicted as active, dominant figures. This reinforcement of stereotypical gender roles can have lasting effects on how individuals perceive their own roles and those of others in society.

For women, the constant exposure to the male gaze can result in feelings of objectification and disempowerment. When women are primarily portrayed as objects of desire, it can be challenging to see themselves as active agents in their own lives. This can impact self-esteem, self-worth, and aspirations.

It may also lead to a culture where women are more likely to be judged based on their appearance rather than their abilities and accomplishments.

Conversely, men may internalize the idea that they should always be in control and that they must conform to a particular masculine ideal. The pressure to conform to these ideals can result in anxiety, depression, and other mental health issues. Men may feel compelled to suppress their emotions and avoid vulnerability, leading to emotional disconnection and strained relationships.

2. Objectification and Its Consequences

At the heart of the male gaze is the objectification of women. Objectification occurs when individuals are reduced to their physical attributes, stripping them of their humanity and agency. This dehumanizing process has serious consequences, both on an individual and societal level.

Women who experience objectification often report lower self-esteem and body image dissatisfaction. They may engage in self-surveillance and self-objectification, constantly monitoring their appearance to conform to societal standards. This can lead to body dysmorphia, eating disorders, and a perpetual sense of inadequacy.

From a societal perspective, the objectification of women perpetuates harmful stereotypes and contributes to a culture of harassment and violence. When women are seen primarily as objects of desire, it becomes easier to justify inappropriate behavior and sexual harassment. This reinforces a culture where women are devalued and their consent is frequently disregarded.

3. Intersectionality: The Multilayered Impact

The impact of the male gaze is not uniform; it varies based on intersecting factors such as race, sexuality, and socioeconomic status. Intersectionality reveals that individuals who belong to multiple marginalized groups face unique challenges and forms of oppression.

For example, women of color often experience a different, more complex form of objectification. They are not only objectified based on their gender but also subjected to racial stereotypes and exoticization. This intersectional objectification can result in a particularly harmful and degrading experience.

Socioeconomic factors also play a role. Women from lower socioeconomic backgrounds may face increased vulnerability to objectification and harassment, as they may have fewer resources to protect themselves or seek legal recourse.

4. Resistance and Resilience

Despite the challenges posed by the male gaze and its intersectional effects, individuals and communities have shown remarkable resilience and resistance. Women and marginalized groups have organized movements, created art, and shared stories that challenge the dominant gaze.

In the face of objectification, many individuals have reclaimed their bodies and narratives, using social media, art, and activism to challenge and subvert the male gaze. These acts of resistance are powerful reminders that individuals have agency and the capacity to redefine their own identities and narratives.

In the following chapters, we'll explore examples of individuals and communities that are actively challenging the male gaze, as well as strategies for promoting media literacy and awareness to combat its harmful effects. It's essential to recognize that while the male gaze may be pervasive, it is not invincible, and change is possible.

Chapter 7:
Breaking Down Stereotypes and Counter-Narratives

In the previous chapters, we delved into the origins and pervasive nature of the male gaze and examined its psychological and societal effects. We have explored how deeply ingrained it is in our culture, from the art of centuries past to contemporary media. However, all is not lost. In this chapter, we turn our attention to the hopeful side of the story—the stories and voices that challenge and subvert the male gaze, offering alternative narratives and representations.

Examples of Media and Art that Challenge the Male Gaze

While the male gaze may dominate much of our media landscape, there are shining examples of creators who actively work to subvert and challenge these norms. These examples often provide us with fresh perspectives, highlighting the importance of diverse voices in storytelling.

1. Film and Television
   - "Wonder Woman" (2017): Directed by Patty Jenkins, this film not only portrays a powerful female superhero but also flips the script on the traditional male gaze. The camera focuses on Wonder Woman's strength and determination rather than objectifying her.

- "Fleabag" (2016-2019): Phoebe Waller-Bridge's groundbreaking series offers a raw and unfiltered look at the life of its titular character, Fleabag. It challenges societal expectations of women and provides a realistic and multi-dimensional portrayal.

2. Advertising
 - Dove's "Real Beauty" Campaign: Dove's campaign challenged conventional beauty standards by featuring women of various body types and ethnicities. It encouraged viewers to redefine beauty beyond the narrow confines of the male gaze.

3. Literature and Writing
 - Roxane Gay's "Bad Feminist" (2014): In this collection of essays, Gay tackles the complexities of modern feminism and critiques media and pop culture through an intersectional lens. Her work encourages readers to question the status quo.

4. Art and Photography
 - Judy Chicago's "The Dinner Party" (1979): Chicago's iconic feminist artwork celebrates the achievements of women throughout history. It challenges the male-centric narratives of history by reclaiming women's stories.

How Marginalized Voices are Reshaping Representations

One of the most exciting developments in recent years is the growing visibility of marginalized voices in the arts and media. Women, people of color, and people with disabilities are increasingly shaping narratives that reflect their experiences.

1. OwnVoices Movement
 - The OwnVoices movement, popularized by author Corinne Duyvis, advocates for stories written by authors who share the same marginalized identities as their characters. This ensures authentic and nuanced portrayals.

2. Intersectionality in Storytelling

- Writers and creators are exploring the intersectionality of identity, recognizing that an individual's experience is shaped by multiple factors, such as race, gender, sexuality, and disability. This approach challenges one-dimensional representations.

3. Social Media and Independent Creators

- Platforms like YouTube, TikTok, and Instagram have provided space for independent creators to challenge traditional narratives. Whether it's makeup tutorials that defy beauty standards or vlogs discussing mental health, these creators have broadened the conversation.

The Power of Storytelling and Diverse Perspectives

Storytelling is a powerful tool for challenging the male gaze. When individuals from diverse backgrounds are given the opportunity to tell their stories, it fosters empathy, understanding, and a richer tapestry of human experiences.

1. Amplifying Personal Narratives

- Personal essays, memoirs, and autobiographical works allow individuals to share their unique experiences. Books like Tara Westover's "Educated" or Malala Yousafzai's "I Am Malala" have opened readers' eyes to different realities.

2. Fiction and Imaginative Works

- Fiction can also challenge the male gaze by creating alternative worlds and narratives. Authors like N.K. Jemisin and Octavia Butler have crafted speculative fiction that challenges traditional gender and power dynamics.

In this chapter, we have seen that the male gaze is not an unassailable force. There are creators, movements, and works that actively challenge and subvert it.

They inspire us to reconsider the way we consume media and view the world around us. However, challenging the male gaze is not without its challenges, and it requires an ongoing commitment to inclusivity and diversity in our media landscape.

In the next chapter, we will shift our focus to the role of feminism and activism in addressing the male gaze, exploring the strategies and initiatives that have been instrumental in pushing for change and progress.

Chapter 8:
The Era of the Me Too Movement

The problem with the male gaze is that seeing women as objects ultimately leads to men believing and feeling like they have the right to engage in sexually related activities with women, even if it is not consensual. Women and girls of all ages face sexual harassment from men. According to RAINN, America's largest anti-sexual violence organization, there is an average of 463,634 victims, 12 years of age or older, of rape and sexual assault every year in the United States. Additionally, an American is assaulted every 68 seconds, and every nine minutes, that victim is a child. Moreover, an estimated 736 million women from around the world aged 15 and above, have been subjected to intimate partner violence, non-partner sexual violence or both at least once in their lifetime. Not to mention the less dangerous but still undermining and bothersome catcalls, whistles and sexual jokes.

"In 2016, 17.7 percent of 10th graders in Washington reported that they had been made to engage in unwanted kissing, sexual touch or intercourse."

-Washington Coalition of Sexual Assault Programs

These statistics show the prevalence of violence and the male gaze in our communities, making it all the more urgent for us to stand up against sexual violence and the toxic patriarchal values that contribute to it.

With sexual harassment and the like being such a widespread issue, it is no surprise that women would band together in creating movements and organizations to combat the harm that is specifically aimed toward females. The Me Too movement took off only a few years ago in 2017, as most people know, due to allegations of sexual assault against media mogul Harvey Weinstein. However, this movement actually started years earlier in 2006 by a woman named Tarana Burke, a survivor of sexual assault.

Me Too has always been about creating change and raising awareness of the impact of sexual violence. Ai-jen Poo, executive director of the National Domestic Workers Alliance stated that:

> *"#MeToo is a movement of survivors and their supporters, powered by courage, determined to end sexual violence and harassment."*
>
> *-Vox.com*

Sexism, misogyny, objectification and all forms of sexual misconduct are still deeply entrenched within the American system, but the Me Too movement has been working to fight against all of that and more by uprooting corrupt men from positions of power, effectively disrupting the male gaze. Many states have passed additional laws helping/protecting victims and survivors and made life-changing reforms. On top of that, American citizens are beginning to take serious action against the power imbalance between genders.

For one, some states have provided more protections against sexual harassment for independent contractors and domestic workers. Federal sexual harassment laws usually only apply to employees, which means that the self-employed freelance writer, Uber driver or makeup artist may have nowhere to turn to for help and/or justice. Furthermore, farm workers, housekeepers, child caretakers and other domestic workers receive little to no sexual harassment protections because they work for employers with 15 or less employees. But in 2018, New York broadened its sexual harassment law to cover independent contractors, and in 2019 improved protections for domestic workers.

States have also banned nondisclosure agreements that include sexual harassment. With Weinstein, he had employees sign an agreement that prevented them from telling anyone about the times he acted inappropriately toward them, which kept many women from speaking up until years later. These types of agreements are harmful, unfair, and to put it bluntly, inhumane. They allow wealthy people to act without consequences while victims must suffer in silence for who knows how long.

As the Me Too movement climbed upwards in popularity, some states passed laws officially forbidding the use of nondisclosure agreements in cases of sexual misconduct. In September of 2018, California, New York and New Jersey enacted these laws. Hopefully, under the new laws, women will be safer and be able to have an easier time speaking up for themselves.

The Me Too movement has also motivated many women and girls to come forward about their experiences with sexual assault.

People who never had any reason to think about sexual assault/harassment before were suddenly thrust into the realization that cases of sexual harassment were not a rare occasion as their friends, family members or coworkers found the courage to disclose their stories to them. Americans' views surrounding sexual harassment began to shift, as can clearly be seen during the Kavanaugh trial. Supreme Court Justice Brett Kavanaugh was accused of sexual assault by Christine Blasey Ford. According to PerryUndem, a research firm, 50 percent of voters thought more deeply about the imbalance of power in government, with men holding more positions than women, after Kavanaugh's hearings. Even if you have never actively harmed or made an inappropriate move towards a woman, that does not mean you are exempt from upholding male-centered ideals. Looking the other way when someone is harassing or committing a crime against a woman is still reinforcing the male gaze.

Former USA gymnastics team doctor and Michigan State University sports medicine physician Larry Nassar was sentenced to between 40 and 175 years in prison for sexually abusing more than 100 young female athletes. Although Nassar was the one physically executing the crimes, officials at the university were also criticized and deemed villainous for ignoring athletes' reports and continuing to enable Nassar. In the end, the university managed to create a $500 million settlement fund for survivors to get financial restitution.

The Me Too movement has yet to make any real, substantial changes to the systemic problems plaguing our society, but its impact has certainly pushed more corrupt men to face the necessary consequences and brought more women up.

Chapter 9: The Role of Feminism and Activism

In the battle against the male gaze, feminism and activism have emerged as powerful weapons of resistance. This chapter delves into the essential role that feminist movements and various forms of activism play in dismantling the entrenched structures of the male gaze.

The Feminist Response

Feminism, with its diverse and evolving ideologies, has been at the forefront of challenging the male gaze. From its earliest waves to the contemporary intersectional feminism, feminist movements have consistently questioned and deconstructed the objectification and subjugation of women perpetuated by the male gaze.

One of the core feminist responses to the male gaze has been the critique of objectification. Feminists argue that the male gaze reduces women to mere objects of desire, stripping them of agency and autonomy. This dehumanization is evident in media, advertising, and popular culture, where women's bodies are often used to sell products or convey power dynamics. Feminist thinkers like Simone de Beauvoir and bell hooks have highlighted how this objectification serves to maintain patriarchal power structures.

Campaigns and Initiatives

Over the years, feminist activists and organizations have launched various campaigns and initiatives to combat the male gaze. These efforts aim to raise awareness, challenge stereotypes, and promote more inclusive and diverse representations of women. One notable campaign is the MeToo movement, which not only shed light on the prevalence of sexual harassment but also exposed the toxic influence of the male gaze in workplaces and society.

The representation of women in the media has been a central concern for feminist activists. Organizations like the Geena Davis Institute on Gender in Media have conducted extensive research to highlight the underrepresentation of women and the reinforcement of gender stereotypes in film and television. This research has led to industry-wide conversations about the need for more balanced and equitable portrayals.

Media Literacy and Education

One of the key strategies employed by feminist activists is media literacy and education. By empowering individuals to critically analyze media content, they can better understand the ways in which the male gaze operates and make informed choices about the media they consume. Media literacy programs and workshops have been instrumental in this regard.

Feminist scholars like Jean Kilbourne have produced groundbreaking documentaries such as "Killing Us Softly," which explores the objectification of women in advertising. These educational tools have been used in schools and communities to foster discussions about media representation and its impact on societal attitudes.

The Power of Social Media

Social media platforms have provided feminists and activists with a powerful tool for challenging the male gaze. The AskHerMore campaign, for example, emerged during red carpet events to encourage reporters to ask female celebrities substantive questions beyond their appearance. The hashtag NotBuyingIt has been used to call out sexist advertisements and media content, sparking public outrage and forcing companies to reconsider their messaging.

Social media has also given marginalized voices a platform to speak out against the male gaze. Women from various backgrounds have shared their personal stories, experiences, and critiques, fostering a sense of solidarity and amplifying the call for change.

Intersectionality and Inclusivity

As feminism has evolved, so too has the understanding of intersectionality, which acknowledges that individuals may experience multiple forms of oppression simultaneously. Intersectional feminism has broadened the conversation about the male gaze by highlighting how race, class, sexuality, and other factors intersect with gender.

Activists have pushed for more inclusive and intersectional approaches to challenging the male gaze. They recognize that women of color often face unique forms of objectification and erasure. In doing so, feminism has become more responsive to the experiences of a diverse range of individuals and more effective in dismantling the male gaze's harmful effects.

Feminism and activism have played a pivotal role in confronting the male gaze and advocating for more equitable and inclusive representations of gender. These movements have challenged long-standing power structures, critiqued objectification, and harnessed the power of media literacy and social media to effect change. By embracing intersectionality and fostering inclusivity, feminist activism continues to shape the conversation and drive progress towards a world where the male gaze no longer holds sway over our perceptions and aspirations.

Chapter 10: Fetishizing Women

The male gaze takes on a slightly different signification when it is directed to women of color. It is different because along with the objectificaton of women, racial stereotypes and inaccurate expectations regarding sex are thrown into the mix as well, while white women do not experience this next level of historical oppression. Racial fetishization occurs when an individual seeks out a person or culture that belongs to a certain race for sexual gratification. The fetishization of women of color is dehumanizing and belittles them down to objects that exist for the sole purpose of fulfilling the male gaze.

In the United States especially, where the country is full of immigrants from differing areas of the world, racial fetishization is highly common. It dates back to a time before the slave trade. White women were viewed as pure and innocent beings who needed to be protected from becoming tainted by Black men. Black women were considered to be full of lust and sin, so white men often objectified them as sexual beings because of the way they looked and what they wore. Black female slaves were raped by white slave owners who saw them as property they could do whatever they wanted with. Even after the United States government abolished slavery, Black women continued to be treated unfairly and thought of as overly sexual beings.

Black female artists today such as Nicki Minaj, Cardi B, and Megan Thee Stallion who empower females by owning their sexuality through their music are heavily criticized. This is because their actions do not fit in line with the expectations society has for them. They are taking power away from the male gaze and putting power into their own hands by wanting to change the way they are perceived.

> *"We never address how cisheterosexual men's sexuality facilitates some unhealthy practices that we've normalized and accepted. Negative reactions to Cardi B result from how, historically, strippers were the objects rather than the subjects of the songs written from the vantage point of a male rapper's voyeuristic and pornagraphic gaze."*
> *-Melissa Brown, Blackfeminisms.com*

Like Black women, Asian women are hypersexualized as well, but not in the same way. While Black girls are oversexualized because they might be thought of as more grown and mature, Asian women are portrayed as childlike and submissive. The U.S military has gone to war many times with Asia, which further perpetuates the idea that Asia, or Asian women, is something to take over or dominate. In addition, the American GIs often participate in the sex industry in countries like Japan, Korea, and Vietnam. As a result, America has come to associate Asian women with sex workers when in reality, there is no specific race or ethnicity that is more likely than others to partake in sex work.

"Asian women are seen as naturally inclined to serve men sexually and are also thought of as slim, light-skinned and small, in adherence to Western norms of femininity."
—Andrea Lim, The New York Times

This modern day view of Asian women can be traced all the way back to The Page Act of 1875, which was the first restrictive federal immigration law in the United States. This law is lesser known compared to its successor, the Chinese Exclusion Act of 1882, which prohibited all Chinese immigrants from entering the United States. The Page Act stopped the immigration of laborers from "China, Japan or any Oriental country" who were brought against their will or for "immoral purposes," with the latter being emphasized much more.

Consequently, it worked to effectively ban East Asian women from coming to the country under the assumption that they were all sex workers. This is a harmful history, especially when Asian women are still hypersexualized and suffering from its effects today. The recent increase in violence toward the Asian American community, such as the Atlanta shooting, can be seen as a direct effect of men's hypersexualization of Asian women.

The portrayal of female sexuality is often not used for character or plot development but as a way to satisfy male/heterosexual viewers with hot and steamy scenes. Unnecessarily long sex scenes tend to focus on the physical acts of the women rather than their emotions or how they are feeling.

Overall, our society's perspectives regarding women are learned from the type of media we absorb and watch on a daily basis. The film industry, and all industries in general, need to stop catering to the male gaze by displaying misleading images falsely representing women of color.

Chapter 11:
Beyond Gender: Intersectionality and the Male Gaze

In the previous chapters, we've explored the insidious influence of the male gaze on the portrayal of women in media and art, and its profound impact on societal perceptions. However, it's essential to recognize that gender is just one facet of identity, and the male gaze intersects with various other factors, such as race, sexuality, and socio-economic status. In this chapter, we delve into the intricate web of intersectionality, examining how these intersecting identities shape and complicate the male gaze narrative.

The Intersections of Race and the Male Gaze

Race and gender are intimately intertwined in the experience of the male gaze. Women of color often face unique challenges, as they navigate both racial and gendered stereotypes simultaneously. Historically, media representations have perpetuated exoticization, fetishization, and the reinforcement of harmful stereotypes about non-white women.

For instance, the hypersexualization of Black women in media has a long and troubling history.

The intersection of the male gaze with racial biases has resulted in the objectification of Black women's bodies, perpetuating harmful myths about their sexuality. This intersectionality not only impacts how Black women are depicted but also affects their self-esteem and body image.

Asian women have also been subjected to stereotypes rooted in the male gaze, often portrayed as submissive and exotic. These stereotypes can have far-reaching consequences, influencing not only how Asian women are perceived but also how they perceive themselves.

Intersectionality adds layers of complexity to the issue of the male gaze. Understanding how gender, race, sexuality, and gender identity intersect allows us to grasp the full scope of this problem and its far-reaching consequences. To address the male gaze comprehensively, we must recognize and challenge its impact on individuals with intersecting identities, striving for media and art that authentically represents the rich diversity of human experiences. This requires not only acknowledging the existence of intersectionality but actively working to dismantle the systems that perpetuate the harmful aspects of the male gaze for marginalized communities.

Chapter 12: Redefining Masculinity

The male gaze doesn't just affect women; it also impacts men and their understanding of masculinity. In this chapter, we'll explore how the male gaze influences men and how redefining masculinity can help break free from its constraints.

The Impact of the Male Gaze on Men

Society has long perpetuated a narrow and rigid view of masculinity, heavily influenced by the male gaze. Men are often pressured to conform to ideals that objectify women and view them as objects of desire rather than individuals with their own agency and worth. This not only harms women but also limits men's emotional expression and self-perception.

The male gaze can foster toxic masculinity, which encourages dominance, aggression, and emotional suppression. Men who embrace this toxic masculinity may struggle with intimacy, empathy, and authentic self-expression. They may also feel the need to constantly prove their masculinity by objectifying women or engaging in harmful behaviors.

Breaking Free from Toxic Masculinity

To challenge the male gaze, it's essential to redefine masculinity. This involves acknowledging that masculinity can be diverse, multifaceted, and, most importantly, healthy. Here are some key steps to breaking free from toxic masculinity:

1. Embrace Vulnerability: Men should be encouraged to express their emotions and vulnerability without fear of judgment. Vulnerability doesn't diminish masculinity; it enriches it.

2. Reject Objectification: Men can actively challenge objectification by recognizing and speaking out against it in media, advertising, and everyday interactions.

3. Promote Respectful Relationships: Promoting respectful and egalitarian relationships is crucial. Men should be allies in the fight for gender equality, supporting women's rights and dignity.

4. Educate and Reflect: Men should engage in self-reflection and educate themselves about the harmful impact of the male gaze and toxic masculinity. Understanding these issues is the first step toward change.

Positive Masculinity and Allyship

Positive masculinity is a concept that encourages men to embody traits like empathy, compassion, and respect for others. It emphasizes cooperation over competition and collaboration over domination. Positive masculinity also recognizes that a man's identity is not threatened by the success or empowerment of women.

Men can become allies in the struggle against the male gaze by actively challenging it in their own lives and communities.

Allyship involves:

- **Listening and Learning:** Actively seeking to understand the experiences and perspectives of women and marginalized communities.

- **Using Privilege for Good:** Using one's privilege to create a more equitable society, whether by advocating for women's rights, supporting gender-inclusive policies, or confronting sexist behaviors.

- **Being Accountable:** Holding oneself and other men accountable for sexist attitudes and behaviors. This includes calling out harmful comments or actions when they occur.

- **Promoting Positive Role Models:** Celebrating and promoting positive male role models who embody healthy masculinity and champion gender equality.

Real-Life Examples of Redefining Masculinity

Throughout history and in contemporary society, there are inspiring examples of men redefining masculinity and challenging the male gaze:

- **Feminist Allies:** Men like Harry Styles, Terry Crews, and Matt McGorry have used their platforms to advocate for gender equality and challenge traditional masculinity.

- **Men's Support Groups:** Organizations like "Men Can Stop Rape" and "A Call to Men" provide resources and support for men seeking to break free from toxic masculinity.

- **Men in Caregiving Roles:** Men who embrace caregiving roles, whether as stay-at-home fathers or nurses, challenge traditional gender norms and show that nurturing is not exclusive to women.

-

Redefining masculinity is a critical aspect of dismantling the male gaze and creating a more equitable society. Men can play a pivotal role in this transformation by rejecting toxic masculinity, embracing positive masculinity, and becoming allies in the fight against objectification and sexism. By doing so, men can help create a world where gender is not a limiting factor, but a source of strength and diversity. In the process, we all benefit from a more inclusive and empathetic society where individuals are valued for who they are, not how they conform to gender stereotypes.

Chapter 13:
The Future of Representation

In our journey through the landscape of the male gaze, we've explored its historical roots, its pervasive presence in art and media, its psychological and societal effects, and the ongoing efforts to challenge and deconstruct it. But where do we go from here? What does the future hold for the way we represent and perceive gender in our society?

The future of representation is a dynamic and ever-evolving space, shaped by technology, shifting cultural norms, and the tireless efforts of activists and artists alike. In this chapter, we will delve into emerging trends and possibilities, examining the potential for more inclusive and diverse representations that go beyond the confines of the male gaze.

Emerging Trends in Media and Art

The digital age has ushered in a new era of storytelling and representation. With the advent of virtual reality (VR), augmented reality (AR), and interactive media, creators have unprecedented opportunities to engage with audiences in novel and immersive ways. These technologies can be harnessed to break free from traditional representations shaped by the male gaze.

Imagine a VR experience that allows you to step into the shoes of characters from diverse backgrounds, genders, and orientations. This level of immersion can foster empathy and understanding, challenging preconceived notions and biases. It offers a tantalizing glimpse into the future of representation, where consumers become active participants in the narrative.

Furthermore, the democratization of media production through platforms like YouTube, TikTok, and social media has enabled marginalized voices to gain visibility. Anyone with a smartphone and an internet connection can now share their stories, perspectives, and talents with the world. This has resulted in a proliferation of content that challenges the status quo and promotes diverse representations.

Breaking Down Barriers

The future of representation is also about breaking down traditional barriers. The line between high art and popular culture is blurring, allowing for more inclusive narratives to reach wider audiences. Independent films, web series, and graphic novels have emerged as powerful mediums for telling stories that challenge the male gaze.

One particularly exciting development is the rise of intersectional storytelling. Creators are increasingly recognizing that individuals do not exist in isolation; their identities are shaped by a complex interplay of factors, including race, sexuality, gender identity, and more. By weaving these intersectional experiences into narratives, we move closer to a more accurate reflection of the diverse world we inhabit.

The Power of Fandom and Activism

The future of representation is inextricably linked to the power of fandom and activism. Fans of various media are demanding change, holding creators and studios accountable for their representations. Social media campaigns, hashtag movements, and organized protests have reshaped the landscape of representation.

For instance, the "OscarsSoWhite" movement, which began as a hashtag on Twitter, shed light on the lack of racial diversity in the film industry and led to meaningful discussions and policy changes.

Strategies for Challenging the Male Gaze in the Digital Age

As we look to the future, it's crucial to equip ourselves with strategies for challenging the male gaze in the digital age. Media literacy programs that teach critical thinking skills are essential to help individuals deconstruct and analyze representations in the media they consume. By understanding the power dynamics at play, audiences can become more discerning consumers and advocates for change.

Additionally, creators and industry professionals must continue pushing for diversity both in front of and behind the camera. This includes hiring more women, people of color, and individuals from underrepresented backgrounds in all aspects of media production. It also involves providing mentorship and opportunities for emerging talent.

—

The future of representation is a tantalizing realm of possibilities.

It's a place where technology, creativity, and activism converge to challenge the limitations of the male gaze. As we navigate this territory, it's important to remember that the future is not predetermined; it's shaped by our collective actions and choices. By actively engaging with and challenging the male gaze, we can work toward a world where diverse representations are not the exception but the norm. This is a future where everyone's stories are valued and celebrated, regardless of gender, race, or identity.

Chapter 14: The Female Gaze

The female gaze is quite the opposite of the male gaze. However, it is not a direct opposite, meaning it does not push for objectification and up close shots of male body parts like washboard abs, rippling, muscular biceps and rock-hard pecs like the male gaze does to women. Instead, it is more about using a female perspective on screen to make the audience feel what women see and experience.

"I find the female gaze easier to define in terms of what it isn't than what it is: it's not about objectifying the female form or replacing fully-realised female characters with loose avatars for male sexual fantasy; it's not framing sex scenes with tropes common to pornography aimed at men; it's not about automatically relinquishing power and control to men in storytelling."
-Phil de Semlyen, Bbc.com

The female gaze sees all people as people rather than objects. It is more emotional, intimate, and filled with empathy. But because of the dominant male gaze in the media, the female gaze has not had a chance to truly spread its wings and take off. The Film Society at Lincoln Center writes, "Few jobs on a movie set have been as historically closed to women as that of the cinematographer. The persistence of the term 'cameraman' says it all."

According to Vulture magazine, the co-director of the documentary Aileen: Life and Death of a Serial Killer, Joan Churchill, details the sensitivity that women bring to the on-screen experience. She also takes note of the fact that men rarely shoot close to people. Instead of being more intimate, they tend to hang back on the sidelines while women are not afraid to step into the thick of things and get close to people. The female gaze also allows diversity and different perspectives into subjects like sexual violence, where women are the most common victims. The way sexual violence is currently being presented on screens through a more decidedly female gaze, emphasizes the urgency of ending sexual violence and the pain of women survivors. Through the female gaze, audiences actually learn a lot more and see a lot more depth than if sexual violence were viewed through the male gaze.

While Mulvey has been deemed the founder and creator of the term "male gaze," French journalist Iris Brey is popular for her book on the female gaze called *The Female Gaze: A Revolution on the Screen* or *Le regard féminin: une révolution à l'écran* in French. Her book garnered quite a bit of attention from the media. Brey is an accomplished academic and a critic for well-known publications such as *Marie Claire* and she is regarded as a prominent feminist thinker. She is also a member of France's 50/50 Collective and a lecturer at the University of California's Paris campus.

In her book, she reveals six criteria that a film must meet to be considered existing within the female gaze and make the audience feel as if they are personally experiencing the female body on screen.

It is necessary that the main character of the film identifies as a woman, that the story is told from her point of view and that her story challenges or calls into question the patriarchal system. The film must be created in a way that allows the audience to feel the female experience, pleasure of the audience must not be derived from objectifying a person in the film and lastly, if there are sex scenes and bodies are eroticized, they must be done so in a conscious manner with a deeper purpose. Brey also makes sure to detail what the female gaze is not. For instance, she does not refer to all films created/directed by women as containing the female gaze. This would make an inaccurate assumption that a director's gender correlates directly with the types of films he or she makes. Just as Black filmmakers do not always make movies centered on race, female filmmakers do not always focus on women. Men can make female gaze films as well.

An example of a film that checks all the boxes when it comes to an accurate portrayal of an empowering female gaze is *Portrait of a Lady on Fire*, a period drama from the French filmmaker Céline Sciamma. It was released in February of 2020 and received ten nominations for the Césars, which are like the French version of the Oscars. The film is set in the 18th century and follows a painter named Marianne, who must complete a portrait in secrecy of a noblewoman named Héloïse. Héloïse had refused to pose for portraits as an act of protest and rebellion against her approaching arranged marriage. What brings out the female gaze is that in order to paint Héloïse in secret, Marianne must memorize each aspect of her features as they go on walks together.

This requires Marianne to look intensely upon Héloise, and the kicker is that Héloise eventually returns her gaze unabashedly. Ginette Vincendeau, a professor of film studies at King's College London, comments on how Marianne and Héloise's relationship provides a blueprint for what the female gaze should look like in cinema and that their relationship is also the very picture of "the reciprocity of the female gaze."

> *"There's more of an equal power relation between the person depicted and the person depicting, which is to me a feminist gesture."*
> *-The Guardian*

Portrait of a Lady on Fire is heavily concerned with appearances and even includes a brief scene of lovemaking, but it does so in a way that manages to avoid focusing on superficial aspects of women's bodies and instead looks beyond that. The film does not emphasize the sex by making the scene needlessly long, including a full-frontal shot of their naked bodies, or pan in on body parts. It focuses on the characters themselves and their emotions, bringing the women's feelings to the forefront of the film. This shows how powerful the female gaze can really be. Where the male gaze creates a narrative that shows women as sexy all the time, the female gaze is showing how women really are: humans with complex thoughts, experiences and emotions who are capable of giving much more to the world than is expected from them. They are more than just bodies, they don't look or feel sexy all the time, and that's okay because that's what is realistic.

Brey argues that the female gaze has a long and rich history;

however, some film experts believe that the female gaze is so new and underdeveloped that they claim the female gaze does not even exist. Natasha Braier, an Argentinian cinematographer, leans more towards the idea of there not being a female gaze. She explains: "I don't think there is such a thing as the female gaze. I think there is such a thing as the male gaze, as per Laura Mulvey's theory, and that gaze, if you talk strictly about cinema only, has more than 100 years of monopoly. It colonized the new medium from the start. You could say that it has become the official language of cinema. The female gaze, if there is such, never had the opportunity to truly develop and become something we can analyze. I think every cinematographer has their own unique gaze, technical skills, and style regardless of their gender. And reducing things to two types of gaze doesn't make much sense to me."

The Female Gaze: A Revolution on the Screen is a book that is one of the first of its kind to make a lasting effort to define and explain the female gaze. The female gaze is a term that induces excitement when mentioned because it represents progress and new ways of thinking.

Chapter 15:
A Gaze into the Future – Breaking Free from the Shackles of the Male Gaze

As we conclude this journey through the intricate landscapes of art, media, and society, it is evident that the male gaze has left an indelible mark on our collective consciousness. We have dissected its origins, traced its progression, and scrutinized its pervasive influence across various facets of our lives. But now, as we stand at the threshold of a new era, it is time to gaze into the future, to imagine a world where the male gaze no longer holds sway, where representations are inclusive, diverse, and emancipatory.

The male gaze, rooted in centuries of patriarchal traditions, has woven a web of objectification, stereotyping, and inequality. However, as we have explored in the preceding chapters, the resistance to this gaze is palpable, and it is growing stronger with each passing day. It is vital to recognize that dismantling the male gaze is not a quest to vilify men or belittle their experiences. Instead, it is an effort to deconstruct harmful narratives and create a world where all individuals, regardless of their gender, can be seen as complex, multi-dimensional beings.

We will reflect on the lessons learned, the potential pathways forward, and the urgency of our collective responsibility in shaping a future free from the constraints of the male gaze.

Lessons Learned

Our journey began with the acknowledgment of the male gaze's existence and its historical foundations. We delved into the artistry of the Renaissance, where women were often reduced to objects of desire and passive muses. We navigated through the annals of film and television, where the male gaze permeated every frame, defining beauty, sexuality, and identity. We uncovered the psychological and societal consequences of this gaze, observing how it perpetuated harmful stereotypes and fostered a culture of objectification.

Amidst this exploration, we discovered the power of resistance. We encountered artists, activists, and everyday individuals who challenged the status quo, who dared to reimagine the world through diverse lenses. From redefining masculinity to championing intersectionality, their stories illuminated a path forward, a path that invites all of us to participate in the transformation of our culture.

The Path Forward

As we tread this path forward, it is crucial to recognize that challenging the male gaze is not a one-size-fits-all endeavor. It requires a multipronged approach that engages individuals, institutions, and entire societies.

Firstly, media literacy must be promoted vigorously. Education is a formidable tool in dismantling the male gaze. When individuals are equipped with the critical skills to deconstruct media messages, they become less susceptible to harmful stereotypes and more discerning consumers of content. Media literacy programs, both in schools and for adults, can empower individuals to challenge the status quo.

Moreover, the media industry itself must undergo transformation. Content creators, producers, and decision-makers hold immense power in shaping narratives. Embracing diversity in all its forms, both in front of and behind the camera, can pave the way for more inclusive representations. Initiatives like the inclusion rider, which advocates for diversity in casting and crew, are promising steps toward change.

Additionally, we must address the larger cultural context in which the male gaze thrives. Patriarchy, toxic masculinity, and rigid gender norms are all intertwined with the perpetuation of the gaze. By promoting healthy masculinity and fostering open dialogue about gender, we can challenge the roots of the problem.

The advent of digital media and the democratization of content creation also offer hope. Social media platforms have given marginalized voices a platform to be heard and have allowed for grassroots movements that challenge the male gaze. The MeToo movement, for instance, has shed light on the pervasive nature of sexual harassment and assault and sparked conversations about consent and power dynamics.

Our Collective Responsibility

As we gaze into the future, we must acknowledge our collective responsibility in dismantling the male gaze. Each one of us has a role to play, whether as consumers, creators, or advocates for change.

Consumers can vote with their views, supporting content that breaks free from the male gaze and rejecting media that perpetuates harmful stereotypes. They can also engage in conversations with friends and family, raising awareness about the issue and promoting media literacy.

Creators, be they writers, directors, artists, or influencers, hold immense power in shaping culture. They must recognize their responsibility to create content that reflects the diversity of the human experience. This may require challenging industry norms and pushing boundaries, but it is a necessary step toward progress.

Advocates and activists are on the frontlines of change, pushing for policies, campaigns, and initiatives that challenge the male gaze. They are organizing protests, starting conversations, and holding institutions accountable. Their work is essential in creating a world where the gaze no longer defines our perceptions of gender and identity.

The male gaze is a formidable adversary, deeply entrenched in our culture. However, it is not invincible. Through education, media transformation, cultural shifts, and individual activism, we can challenge and ultimately dismantle the male gaze. The stories of resistance and transformation we have explored in this book remind us that change is possible, and the future is not bound by the limitations of the past.

As we move forward, let us envision a world where every gaze, regardless of the gender from which it emanates, is a gaze of respect, empathy, and understanding. Let us work tirelessly to create a society where the full spectrum of human experiences is celebrated, where individuals are seen not as objects, but as equals. This vision may seem ambitious, but it is a vision worth pursuing. Together, we can break free from the shackles of the male gaze and usher in an era of true equality and representation for all.

The Bottom Line

While we have become more aware of the male gaze and the disgusting ideas it propagates, we are also equipped with enough knowledge to not buy into it. It is sad to say that such depictions of women are a normal part of our popular culture and society. Cat calling, stalking women on or after getting off of public transportation, gawking at women in line, "accidentally" touching women inappropriately, etc. All of these are unconsciously inspired by the male gaze portrayed on screen.

Mulvey and Menkes have shone a light on the repetitive style of cinema we see on a daily basis, and their ideologies have displayed a truthful version of cinema that gives a more accurate portrayal of women now more than ever before. For example, the *Hunger Games* franchise brings a fresh take on how a girl, Katniss Everdeen, can stand up for herself without the need for a man to be at her side at all times. After the death of her father, where he left behind a family of women, Katniss is able to take on the more "masculine" duties of hunting and trading at the black market without the help of a male figure. Katniss is also clearly aware of her objectification throughout the different stages of her life under the Capitol and she eventually strives to do something about it.

She at first refers to herself as "a piece in their Games," and realizes how she is being objectified once more as the tributes are forced into costumes and prance around for show during the opening ceremonies. When she holds out the poisonous berries in the arena in defiance of the Capitol, she is showing how she is aware of the Capitol's control, how she cannot be controlled, and how she simply does not want to be controlled. She refuses to play by the rules the Capitol has enforced, just as the male gaze enforces a set of rules to view and depict women by.

An independent female protagonist, capable of being the sole provider for her family, of fending for herself, of murder, and of taking down an entire empire almost singlehandedly, is definitely grounds for a narrative told through the female gaze. Thus, this does not leave readers feeling as if the main character has been objectified and does not show her in the same light as portrayed in the Male Gaze.

And we are just scratching the surface because there is still so much to discover and understand about the male gaze. Do we get rid of the male gaze altogether or just try to redefine the male gaze? If so, how? Will the female gaze ever be prioritized and earn its rightful place in the media? Are the gazes limited to just two—male and female—or are there more? Will women of color ever stop experiencing a perverse fetishization upheld by men?

Although we still have a long way to go in terms of empowering women in all areas of life and society, it is safe to say that the male gaze is becoming less pervasive. Women are breaking into once-forbidden roles and attaining higher positions of power. They are speaking up, and their voices are actually being heard. With more women in leadership positions, there is a better chance that the female gaze will prevail.

Acknowledgments

Writing a book is a journey that rarely, if ever, happens in isolation. It is a culmination of countless hours of research, reflection, and creativity. I am deeply grateful to the many people and organizations that have played a pivotal role in bringing this book, "Unveiling the Gaze: Challenging the Male Gaze in Art, Media, and Society," to life.

First and foremost, I want to express my heartfelt gratitude to my family for their unwavering support and understanding throughout this journey. Your patience, encouragement, and belief in me have been my constant source of inspiration. To my parents, who instilled in me a love for learning and a passion for equality, I owe an immeasurable debt of gratitude.

I extend my deepest appreciation to my academic advisors, mentors, and colleagues who have guided me through this project. Your expertise, feedback, and willingness to engage in insightful discussions have enriched the content of this book. I'd like to acknowledge [Name of Advisor/Mentor], whose wisdom and mentorship have been instrumental in shaping my ideas and sharpening my critical thinking.

To the numerous scholars, activists, and artists whose work forms the backbone of this book, I express my profound gratitude.

Your pioneering efforts to challenge the male gaze and redefine gender representations in art and media have paved the way for a more inclusive and equitable world. Your contributions to the field have not only informed this book but have also ignited a flame within me to continue the pursuit of justice and equality.

I would also like to thank the interviewees who generously shared their personal experiences and insights. Your stories have added depth and authenticity to this work. Your courage in confronting the challenges of the male gaze is a testament to the resilience of the human spirit.

This book would not have been possible without the support of [Publisher's Name]. I am grateful for their belief in the importance of this topic and their commitment to amplifying diverse voices. The editorial team, designers, and production staff have been instrumental in shaping this book into its final form.

I want to acknowledge the tireless efforts of my research assistants, whose dedication to the project helped gather valuable data, conduct interviews, and compile resources. Your commitment to this cause is commendable, and your contributions have been invaluable.

I am indebted to the countless organizations and activists working tirelessly to challenge the male gaze and promote gender equality. Your advocacy, campaigns, and initiatives are making a tangible difference in our society. I encourage readers to engage with and support these organizations, as their work is essential in reshaping our cultural landscape.

To my friends and peers who provided moral support, encouragement, and a listening ear during the ups and downs of the writing process, I am deeply grateful. Your belief in this project has kept me motivated and focused.

I must also extend my appreciation to the broader community of researchers, writers, and advocates who are dedicated to addressing issues of gender representation and inequality. Your ongoing work inspires and reinforces the importance of this book's message.

Lastly, I want to express my gratitude to the readers of this book. Your interest in exploring the complexities of the male gaze and your commitment to fostering a more inclusive society are deeply appreciated. It is my hope that this book serves as a catalyst for meaningful discussions and positive change.

I am reminded of the African proverb, "It takes a village to raise a child." In a similar vein, it takes a community of support, collaboration, and shared purpose to bring a book to fruition. Each person mentioned here and countless others not named have contributed to this endeavor in their unique way. I am honored to have been a part of this collective effort to challenge the male gaze and promote a more equitable world.

Thank you all for your unwavering support, dedication, and belief in the power of words to effect change. This book stands as a testament to our shared commitment to a more inclusive and just society.

With deepest gratitude,

Liz Fe

Appendix

In your journey to understand and address the complexities of the male gaze and its impact on gender representation, you'll find a wealth of resources, both scholarly and accessible, that offer valuable insights, analysis, and perspectives. This curated list encompasses a variety of books, articles, documentaries, and organizations that delve deeper into this critical subject matter.

Books

1. "The Second Sex" by Simone de Beauvoir: This groundbreaking work explores the history of women's oppression and provides foundational ideas for feminist thought.

2. "The Beauty Myth" by Naomi Wolf: Wolf investigates the societal pressure on women to conform to beauty standards and the consequences of this pressure.

3. "Visual Pleasure and Narrative Cinema" by Laura Mulvey: This seminal essay introduced the concept of the male gaze in cinema, analyzing how it operates and impacts storytelling.

4. "Killing Us Softly: Advertising's Image of Women" by Jean Kilbourne: A comprehensive examination of how advertising perpetuates gender stereotypes and objectification.

5. "Men Explain Things to Me" by Rebecca Solnit: Solnit's essays tackle the issue of male condescension and how it manifests in everyday life.

6. "Hood Feminism: Notes from the Women That a Movement Forgot" by Mikki Kendall: A critical exploration of mainstream feminism's shortcomings and the importance of intersectionality.

7. "Reel Inequality: Hollywood Actors and Racism" by Nancy Wang Yuen: Investigates racial disparities in Hollywood and the representation of Asian actors.

8. "Amazons, Wives, Nuns, and Witches: Women and the Catholic Church in Colonial Brazil, 1500-1822" by Carole A. Myscofski: Explores the intersection of gender, religion, and power in colonial Brazil.

Articles and Essays

1. "The Male Gaze: Understanding Its Impact on Our Culture" - A comprehensive article discussing the history and implications of the male gaze in media and society.

2. "The Intersectionality Wars" by Jane Coaston: This Vox article delves into the complexities of intersectionality and its role in feminist discourse.

3. "The Problem with the 'Strong Female Character'" by Tasha Robinson: A thought-provoking essay that challenges the superficial portrayal of women in media.

4. "Toxic Masculinity: The Male Gaze and Its Impact on Men" - An exploration of how the male gaze can harm men by reinforcing harmful notions of masculinity.

Documentaries and Films

1. "Miss Representation" (2011): This documentary examines the underrepresentation and misrepresentation of women in media and politics.

2. "The Mask You Live In" (2015): Explores the societal pressures and expectations placed on boys and young men, including the impact of the male gaze.

3. "Killing Us Softly" series: A collection of documentaries by Jean Kilbourne that dissect the portrayal of women in advertising.

4. "This Film is Not Yet Rated" (2006): Investigates the secretive and often biased process of film censorship and its implications for gender representation.

Organizations and Websites

1. Geena Davis Institute on Gender in Media: A research-based organization focused on increasing gender diversity and reducing stereotypes in media.

2. The Representation Project: The organization behind "Miss Representation," working to challenge and overcome limiting stereotypes in media.

3. Women in Film: A nonprofit organization dedicated to promoting gender parity in the entertainment industry.

4. Everyday Feminism: An online publication that offers articles, courses, and resources on intersectional feminism and social justice.

5. The Bechdel Test: A simple but revealing tool for assessing gender representation in film and other media.

6. The Good Men Project: A platform that explores healthy masculinity and challenges traditional notions of manhood.

This list is by no means exhaustive, but it should provide you with a solid foundation for further exploration of the male gaze and its implications for gender representation. These resources offer a diverse range of perspectives and insights, allowing you to engage deeply with this crucial issue in our society.

References

1. Berger, John. (1972). "Ways of Seeing." Penguin Books.

2. Mulvey, Laura. (1975). "Visual Pleasure and Narrative Cinema." Screen, 16(3), 6-18.

3. Hooks, Bell. (1981). "Ain't I a Woman: Black Women and Feminism." South End Press.

4. Butler, Judith. (1990). "Gender Trouble: Feminism and the Subversion of Identity." Routledge.

5. Dyer, Richard. (1982). "The White Man's Gaze." Screen, 23(3-4), 29-38.

6. Davis, Angela Y. (1981). "Women, Race & Class." Random House.

7. Wolf, Naomi. (1991). "The Beauty Myth: How Images of Beauty Are Used Against Women." Harper Perennial.

8. Bordo, Susan. (1993). "Unbearable Weight: Feminism, Western Culture, and the Body." University of California Press.

9. Butler, Judith. (1993). "Bodies That Matter: On the Discursive Limits of 'Sex'." Routledge.

10. Kilbourne, Jean. (1999). "Deadly Persuasion: Why Women and Girls Must Fight the Addictive Power of Advertising." Free Press.

11. Mulvey, Laura. (2006). "Death 24x a Second: Stillness and the Moving Image." Reaktion Books.

12. hooks, bell. (1992). "Black Looks: Race and Representation." South End Press.

13. Collins, Patricia Hill. (2000). "Black Feminist Thought: Knowledge, Consciousness, and the Politics of Empowerment." Routledge.

14. Dill, Karen E., & Zambrana, Ruth E. (2009). "Blacks' Diminished Sensitivity to the Negative Effects of Television on the Racial Attitudes of Whites." Media Psychology, 12(3), 260-282.

15. McRobbie, Angela. (2004). "Post-Feminism and Popular Culture." Feminist Media Studies, 4(3), 255-264.

16. Valenti, Jessica. (2016). "Sex Object: A Memoir." Dey Street Books.

17. Mitchell, Juliet. (1974). "Psychoanalysis and Feminism: Freud, Reich, Laing, and Women." Vintage.

18. Lorde, Audre. (1984). "Sister Outsider: Essays and Speeches." Crossing Press.

19. Goffman, Erving. (1979). "Gender Advertisements." Harper & Row.

20. hooks, bell. (2000). "Feminism is for Everybody: Passionate Politics." South End Press.

The Toxic Female Gaze

CUE THE 'MEAN GIRLS' REFERENCES
LIZ FE LIFESTYLE

Is the Term Feminism the New "F" Word?

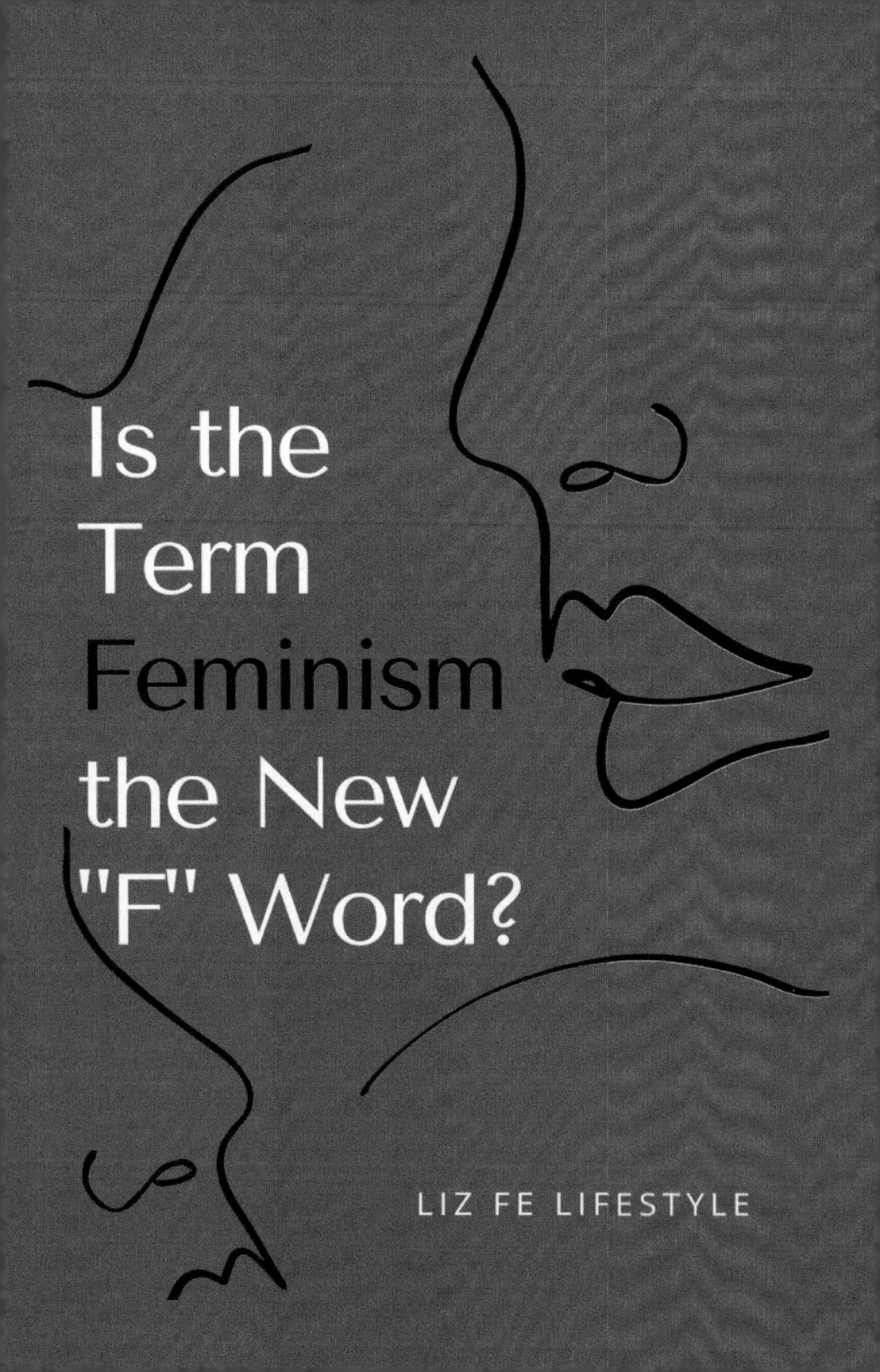

LIZ FE LIFESTYLE

Coming Soon

IF WOMEN DON'T OWE MEN PRETTY, THEN

MEN DON'T OWE WOMEN MONEY

LIZ FE LIFESTYLE

WOMEN WHO HATE WOMEN

LIZ FE LIFESTYLE

Please leave a review for us on Amazon, we really appreciate the support.

LIZ FE LIFESTYLE

Empowered Women Book
Publisher: lizfelifestyle.com

Check Us Out: @LizFeLifestyle